TODD SWIFT

Madness
And Love In
Maida Vale

ON THE OCCASION OF
HIS TURNING 50

First published in 2016
by Eyewear Publishing Ltd
Suite 333, 19-21 Crawford Street
Marylebone, London W1H 1PJ
United Kingdom

Typeset with graphic design by Edwin Smet
Printed in England by Lightning Source

.

ISBN 978-1-911335-03-0

Eyewear wishes to thank Jonathan Wonham for his generous patronage of our press.

WWW.EYEWEARPUBLISHING.COM

Thanks to
all my friends, family, Sooty the cat,
and the memory and reality of Jack, Bev, Melita...
my beloved inspirers when I was young.

Lovers are the ones who
know most about God;
the theologians must listen to them.
– Hans Urs von Balthasar

FOR SARA EGAN

AND HANS VAN DE WAARSENBURG

Table of contents

Christ, swimming

If Christ swam on the cross,
he didn't drown.
He took the wood as a boat.
Water was always good to Christ.
God flooded the world easily.
I don't blame God

for disasters at sea. I do, though
wonder at prayer, at praying,
when it seems God rarely hears.
But back to Christ on his oars,
rowing his lungs back
to crushing his own breathing

down. He drowned on the cross
in the blue air of spring.
But it would have felt like summer
in the heat. He dove into
his crucifixion like it was a lake
clear as a promise to be kind.

To be good. He swam out to
the raft, to cling to the wood
that did him no good, that saves us
somehow. Theology
is the way we puzzle out
the mystery of that swim

up there, in blood and oxygen,
Jesus our fish the Romans caught,
that the crowd threw back,

selecting Barabbas for the feast.
He usually walked on water
but I prefer him doing lengths

of the cross, his arms stretched
in a painful breaststroke.
He suffered doing the crawl
on his lifeguard's chair
they nailed him to for the summer.
I love good Jesus for his distance

swim from God to where
we stood on the sand
waiting for him to come out
of the waves; to rise up and out
like Venus. Beauty saves, but
more truly, for a carpenter, does

a stern and bow, a mast and maidenhead.
Jesus sailed out of the sea of the dead,
His body dripping love for me.
And I am crazy to say so,
but my fideism is such I love the myth
because it may be true, and feels

true when I say it in my mind;
that the one who is most kind
floats free of the wreck's SOS.
This isn't the sombre lies I planned
to plane out, my own crafted object
striving to line up words with need –

but I don't feel you require any pathos
to understand that a carpenter sank
when he took up his woodwork

to break the bank of heaven's clouds
with his calm strong arms;
and the lake of the onlooker's tears

ran like a river of vinegar
into the place where balm and horror
meet. And they never broke
his legs or feet, the soldiers:
he came off his starting block last,
our captain of the swim team.

Mystery Girl Deluxe

It was never quite the kiss or weather.
We fell down after reading together
Simply since love is a matter of fact
At Easter; it often follows the act
Of indiscipline, the shifting feathers
That transform a swan; bars of leather
Were not our scene, but we attacked
Ideas of unison with underage tact.
We ached to wake up as F. Kafka;
Cherry-balmed lips the morning after.
It was sub-zero that April in Montreal;
The metro was blue; the turnstile
Saw us part, Walkmans synchronised
To Orbison's dream tears in our eyes.

April Snow

We have seen Christ in April, or so to speak,
snow has come down, unseasonably.
Unreasonably, also. The fragrance on her wrist.

It is possible to make pronouncements about
the world, and salvation, and keep a straight face,
but you may grimace also. You may flap your arms.

Truth is always under reconsideration, has
a revolving door policy. I like the Truth because
it holds a number of possibilities, like a phone.

You may dial Jesus. You may dial eternal damnation.
Feel free to make of your Self as you will. Others do.
Did you really think I would embrace your nation

without complex feelings? Emotion will out,
as parasols on a sunny day. A radiance floods
the world, even when it is least bright.

This is the radiance called praying for light.
The prayer makes the God come into the picture;
words make the God step out of the wall.

This is the exact opposite to expelling a demon.
You send devils running from pigs with a shake
of the fist, with chicken bones and some hair dye.

You use ritual and a winking eye and language
to make words do things with superstition
they might not want to. You possess words

to repossess the pigs that were taken over by devils.
Anyway, salvation is the other way around.
No spitting or writing on the leathery ground.

Unbind your wrists and ankles, here.
You call God on the phone and he comes over
like a pool cleaner, like a call girl.

You pray to God and then there is a God knocking.
And he does not see you when you answer.
There is too much busyness of need in the world

for anything as simple as the visible realm
to be involved in the creation of fulfilment,
all your desires fed at once, the multiple satiation

of snow petals dropping rapidly in April, unseasonably.
Lightness of fragrance. A slap on the wrist, a kiss
and a promise. A door left half open, and a calling,

almost an orchestration, somewhere above
your eye, summoning the weather
to bow to its own conclusions.

Love Song

They hate love so much
They tend to kill it
With a dart
Drawn straight through
The designated heart.
I have seen dissection tables
In labs where trained
Believers in natural laws
Have torn a gazelle apart.
It feels like that,
The songs say,
Each time it beats fluid out,
Drop by sustained drop;
It is worse than scalpels

At the chest cavity,
Cold as December,
To have love pulled out.
So odd a toxin,
It kills when going in
Worse leaving the body,
Little winged weird killer thing.
But love is also
The dove after slaughter
Who beyond battery
Arrives austere
On Ararat
To sing.

Poems On Unoriginal Themes One: Tattoos

I burnt it off to be like me, again.
I took my skin back to being
A baby, more or less. Spotless,
Milky, not a cast of sin. Tattoo-less

Again was the second new beginning.
She used a laser like in Bond,
I saw the hearts, the dragons,
The names of lovers undo

Their fame. It was like a pond
Freezing over, going all ice-blank.
I began to forget my body's
Debts to those I'd once paid

Honour with this pain of inking.
Half-way through her surgery
I got to thinking, this was erasure
Not of the visible, but the unseen.

The daggers and the bloody crucifix,
The Hindenburg date and Germanic
Signs, the beaded tears and sweat,
The badly-drawn porcupine,

Shelley, Medbh and Anne-Marie –
It wasn't ripping off a simple layer,
But drinking out the dregs of an ID,
So that what I could remember

Would be remapped as pristine.
No good to be so clean, I said.
I broke from that low chair and fled
Fast from her Harley street prison

Hell-bent on getting remade
In the image of all those imagoes,
My spattered insignia to be reapplied
So I could fit into my own job description.

Poems On Unoriginal Themes Two: Twins

He's me except he's not. Like a blood clot
He formed in the blood I gave.
Jesus saves, but I share. He has my hair,
My eyes. He kisses my wife, thoughtlessly.

I see him hesitate at my children's door.
He knocks then shifts away. He's daddy
Minus my limp, my lilt. He's to the hilt
Play-acting the family man and poet,

But he knows very little, and is inadequate.
He's poor at running. Barely can ski.
He slips on skates. Can't cook for beans.
Looks bad in jeans. Is putting on diabetes

As a possibility. He whimpers in the dark.
He has a problematic relationship to cars:
Just see him try to park. And yet, he appears
In mirrors, windows, and photo-montages

As my double. He goes to a lot of effort,
Even trouble, to double tie the knot
At his throat. His eyes are on remote,
But his hands are never care-free.

He's a perfect imitation of who I am,
Minus the best parts, that others admire.
He has no PhD, no engineering nous.
He wasn't on the island that summer, with us.

He owns no patents, none of our stocks.
Until he learns to pick our locks,
Which he will. And then, my very own
Wilson Wilson will no doubt move in,

Usher me out with a surreptitious kill,
A slipping in of the dirk, a kick downstairs,
Perhaps a bag over the breathing apparatus.
I'll be stifled, then dissolved in lye.

He'll slip in between hot sheets, ice-cool.
He'll lie, fool, metamorphose, adroitly,
Into who he always was, in waiting:
My ideal reader, my brother, my editor.

Poems On Unoriginal Themes Three: Ghosts

You see them when you don't.
They have little clout
But wind up the air to scuttle.
They are death's rebuttal,
An after-life riposte.
They burn ethereal toast.
They have no cost, are untaxed.
Ghosts use no wax, which explains

How they squeak like doors
Unhinged. They're rust learning
A new trick. They're dusk
Buttered on too thick.
And the patter of fog tendrils.
I don't want to live with one
Unless the house has a sea-view
And my house-keeper is pale.

But in a family, ghosts are a pain.
They throw plates like any parent
Or child. They're a wilder version
Of love going off the rails,
They're just marriage dialled up a bit.
Poltergeist, meet my wife,
Meet my son, my daughter.
You won't really slaughter us.

I know because the blood is false,
It's melted umber crayon,
And those eyes are cut through mist
As if God's scissors had met gauze.
Ghost, you break the major laws
But never seem to miss a chance
To, on schedule, imbalance
A vase or smash a pane. Ululations

This regular prove amenable
To prediction, hypothesis, science:
We know spirits are supernatural,
But give us natural metaphors
Whenever we need to describe
Spies off the radar, limbs cut away,
Memories on loveless rainy days.
Thank you, ghosts, for being useful,

And, in your hint at immortality,
Oddly comforting, even quaint.
Though when you leap from the telly
A grandmother just may faint.
Ghost, you are soft as drying paint,
A mourner's sighs. A last good-bye.
An infant's cry, icy breeze. Frightful seas.
The snow-white whiteness of Snow White.

Madness And Love In Maida Vale

Ash, Wednesday

My father, in his coffin,
broke any sense
I'd had that life was good.
His stillness,
in the midst of things,
was far too complete
to be much comfort.
God promises some
form of return,
when we walk the streets
marked out as fools
in our desperate hope
we are possessed still
by what cannot die,
what ignites,
the match-head blue
striking of Christ.

For James Brookes

God's silence is not absence, it is omission.
Purely, he punishes us by not intervening.

Jehovah could come like a solar flare, burst
all the power lines, wipe our screens away.

We could be cleansed as the solar wind is,
rising out of its own circles of eruption to stay.

Great Malvern

For my grandfather Stanley Swift

I.

He comes late in the day to the town
near the ancient bare hills,
Blue Bird Café, Christian bookshop,
Elgar statue, and estate agents.
No we cannot drive you to the viewings
because once a woman was killed
that way, meet us at the houses.
You must drive yourself. He doesn't drive.
So he goes without any viewings
about no business there, in the darkening
air of January at four, because
he has no business among these people;
dawdles like a schoolboy in another
shop selling old books sold by the old.
Malvern is dying almost as the sun will,
in stages, first decline then later return.
To discover yourself wander among strangers,
or so he says when in doubt.

2.

It's all sad in a lonely widower way –
his walk back down the long hill
to the station branches endlessly; once
he stopped at a high stone wall, for
a Girl's School, and felt great pressure
on his coat, as if a gale sought to throw
the man he appears to be up among
the silver birches, like a lost exotic bird.

Up in a room of books and music, none
of it of any interest to anyone living now,
he had found himself in a pew, praying
for the dead, as if they could ever know
his needs, which are few, but feel legion.
His needs, really, are sustainable,
and resolve down to an idea of love
formed in that endless long ago
where half the ones he loves are gone,
as if life was a ship always turning over
and letting the old people drown.

3.
His need now was only for a driver to link
Malvern's scattered houses hid among firs;
homes like strangers dispersing after a pause
to hover by the victim on the pooling corner.
No sea or violence here, in this Priory, this shadowed
village under a high bare hill, burnt cold yellow
in the disadvantaged light, lowering into a bath
of darkness, as if it held onto added railings for safety.
The old grow older, the high trees grow stranger,
the absence of any names he recognises
in the whole region make the wells and wildflowers
almost familiar in comparison, the walking trails,
as if he was only a visitor come for the waters
when Shaw might be holding forth with Waugh;
though his grandfather, he was reliably informed,
was born somewhere among these closed doors,
the locked embers of the sun turning off, away.
The sun is the ageing relation who dies one day,
but you remember them again in how you awake
to revisage yourself in a mirror they bequeathed
you in their contested will; but proven

finally to be valid. So it all comes across to you,
the last one of the line, the bare Swift in the bald
tree, broken by a fist of wind, a thrown stone,
small now and flapping with fading ingenuity,
stiffening under the combing fingers of last lights.

4.
No one visits dying birds to offer them last rites,
they wither in anonymity, as icicles pass on
their tendencies to go to another state, ungrieved.
Most of nature swells and spasms uncalled for,
unproclaimed, these hills and their spawn
throb with a kingdom unbannered. It all praises
itself instead, has to look inwards, reclaims
a sense of being birthplace and grave in one
returning circuit, a walk you could do in an hour,
on foot, following the waymarkers, faces
that do not flash with appreciation or recognition –
you are him, and he is entirely abandoned here,
might as well be from another county, or year;
almost that century before the last one, go on
back into the musty folds of half-eaten mothy trim.
It's just being on your own, widowed at eventide,
when the lightship flounders on night rocks.

5.
English has been Germanic in structure
for more than a thousand years, comforting,
though the glaciers that melted on this plain
were tens of thousands older; *the water has nothing
in it*. This is what makes it good said the doctor
who sold the town to the world; absence,
he discovers, losing his way many more times

slowly, is a reminder of goodness. How peace
and silence try to speak our tongue, and fail
nobly. The evening hums with a thought it has
no mode to express, as if locked behind the windows
of the second-hand clothing shops for charities –
for the starving, the prisoners, the cancerous –
we give used things away to what we don't want
to ever be. We lock up what we offer when night
reminds us we are sleeping creatures, at last.
Malvern shuffles to other lighted spaces inside
and the wandering without neighbours,
homeless if only because unhomed, unaddressed,
have no locksmith to open up the evening,
the facades become facades after all. Open
places close, even the Christians lock up
their chocolate cake, which was stale.

6.
At the station the London train sits for hours
and no one comes to board. It is like a play
that failed. Not a dream only, but also a dream,
this unstaged tableau has the momentous
incidents of a less important fantasy, ages
even as it sinks into being a schedule forgotten
to occur; a book without pages; the printer
out of ink and all the settings smashed by a king
who hates to be spoken to by words.
It has a false truce feel to it, a true false truce,
holding a lost love gone back to being found,
in the way that flowers are in and out
of the ground, the way our names carry us
out of our homelands and townships, up
across seas, to places with other names,
and suddenly being called once, by mother,

father, brother, sister, would add range
to the solar fling, silver the paling edges of light;
but no one calls out your name now, not allowed
in case someone might die in the risk
of stepping out to a lost self, identity
has slipped here into the wells and shadows.
No beauty is greater than going about
without purpose, locating a new rental
in the broken down fields, stones where Swifts
once fled and hid among the waterless stars,
in which, not being water, everything is,
our names, our new needs, and the dead,
who will give us a call, and whistle to train
the conductor to send the engines rolling
on gale-force tracks all the way to London.

X: The Man With X-ray Eyes

A doctor without cash
may have to throw his best friend
through a high window
and stumble over barbed wire
to proclaim a dark light
at the burning atomic source;
no man with a tie
should be let go from research
or criminally underfunded
even if the vile eye drops
turn molten gold
and drive mania like nails
into the rational skull;
keenly good at cards;
with a monomaniac's swagger,
Ray Milland was the X-ray Man,
drunk on cheap budgets
and a lost career;
finned car careening from Vegas
and the educated girl; a radiant
hammering ripping of flesh
off the visible bones,
and Les Baxter timpani
and xylophones
vibrating the score;
you see what you desire;
and then you desire more;
and as you plunge architectonic
past creatures of the sea
you zoom in on monstrosities:
skeletal motions

the living resemble
in their stripped down
structures: already dead.
Yet I pity no man handsome
after a sandy car wreck,
dapper with the torn dignity
of a tailored genius scorned
in a world gone mad,
or made manic by money;
your insane vision was to want
what the spying gods have;
and then to rave once
you had seen the blunt sun;
and seen the exposed
negation
of the blatant sun instead,
naked in violent zero of the day.

On The Growing Darkness In My Mind

ashamed, mostly
       for slipping
around emphasis
declensions
I don't know about me
       anymore
I is half an I
closing
vicissitudes
       angers
slammed shut
rages
books torn up inside
       cut lyrics apart
sag
war
forcelessness
       I see myself limp
in a storming
where's shelter
of the brain?
       all's loose
compendium
worse spears
of pain
       angels come to me
I am bedevilled too far
for my wit to contend
friend friend
       I ask for gentleness of mind
god specialist, minder

bend and salve, be good
in my whirlpool
      I can't imagine
more this sort of
unendurable thing could
in such a small vessel
      last
gnash
now is the part of day
bloodblisters
      boils
the sunface off
away staggering
hold something fast
      internal command
I growl to bedlam
to lie down
in bed in growing
      harsh unintelligibilities
light broken like frost
demands pinnacle
winter it is in spring
      I grasp nettles
to balm what stings;
dumb palmistry
all of what thinks
      is thinks is me
is footloose ledger
I am in real danger
come see what thinking has wrought
      upon your son
inheritance
stressors
I bend braniacal, uncovered
      cannot apologise enough

for what's happening
invisible cuts too cute
to handle, no
    repeat, come in
send troops
upon the blossoms now
a stick figure of porcelain snaps
    its biscuit in a tricycle
of anguishing
domain
unflappable
    parlance is the dungeon
where the mast of ferocious
I can't be this person anymore
talks up a rainstorm
    in toe-tapping compliance
with babble gofuck
the dick of it is
I haven't been this lost
    since the canal
whence from therefore hence
all's been sixpence spent
in florid
    entanglements of sorcery
of material tug of war
oh please shut the doortrap
and recall
    I thought I once was
who I never can appear to be
again, in maida vale
mudplain of generous decline
    I forgive you for love
go forth and testify
of plainspeech
embalmistry

the fate of single thoughts
split hairs
burning rubber
tyres spun
too fast
roadworks
engineering sputter
ramble mutter
too thin butter
best left for dead
I will hold
the injuns
off at
the pass
padre
go blow
your nasty snotrag
at the shores
of angelsea
and commitment
lisp latch
close stitch lips
go gore and put
the masons slit
a chicken here
to spout juice
of berries
berry nice to see you
in the choir
even if you sing
like a frog
shot in the good leg
goodluck
sweet jesus
it hurts in the hurricanes

circustry of my dumble
    down stairs topple off
go slow here
I can't manage these flights
of linguistic accoutrement
    so much
since I remembered
I was plotlost
and not sane in the manner
    accustomed to being
held high
dignity dashes
like a customer without the means
    to pay the meal
eat of me
in the tangle of this
agon is a myth
    called lucid
exposition
hold this line
awhile
    I am going for
a walk
where the grass
can speak in
    my mouth
for an earthtime
of swallows

wanting utterance

April 23, 2015

On The Flaggy Shore In Swanlight At 49 At Easter

Feeling like P. Seymour Hoffman
burly against the sunlight in airplanes
heavy as the day is long in spring
an addict, an ageing troubled fatman;

creative division or just lazy psyche,
the anger books pile on – I need
more lives to learn to live this one.
The lying down on sunny flagstones

by the withdrawn tide on the shore
blows my heart open too, Heaney.
49 years to becoming a heathen
by way of Rome; apologetics aside

I am rarely home these days.
The world itself is revelation,
the world's way of being is telling truth;
what is, fragile and surface-tense, flees,

informing us of the fact the world is false;
the world reveals its unreal status
in time, which itself is a constant failing;
nothing inheres or holds, the flux

ruins its own chances. The clouds
are thrown about like seabirds
on the rising seafoam; the crows
and geese dance badly in the wind –

the swans appear bold on a flood;
all is grease and hinge, door and knock.
All is going blind before it goes dark.
Throw a match down a well and hear

fire without an echo, because vision
offers no Helicon; the flagging stones
have held this peninsula for eons;
no change, okay, little change in souls;

addicted to what? Excitations?
The plane judders but doesn't die;
this time the pilot loves his family.
The world itself is murder, it tells

us how what is in the world is destroyed
in time, which is a juggernaut
with no good business on a country lane;
scattering the cyclists, the old walkers.

The world enfolds and opens at once;
it goes about itself like a god
never absent from what it shows;
the world is all revelation; what you see

is what is given, what is tested, on loan.
Burly in the fat air of noon I sleep wingside
and age into my next year; below
is cloud heaven and green ground hope.

There's no resolution in what's me.
I don't have time to learn to cope
with all the strategies that'd have me cope
with all the traumas inflicted 49 times.

Madness And Love In Maida Vale

Each bam bam damn nail in the symbol,
Easter my cross being born just like the rest;
we land, we leave, we go, we train into London.
Alone lonely as alone is allowed; solitary,

mister love myself, master love me for me;
without love the world is only pain;
with pain the world is only love;
level or on a slanting angle, it tells the same;

it calls another name, time runs to another child;
the arms that hold her cannot also lift us.
Go down to the flaggy shore on Easter Monday
and watch the black smear of shore exposed

when the sea has pulled back its foreskin.
No image is good, no phrase is wise;
the world is language; and both lie
on the basis, of which they express

their nature; which is flimsy; solidman,
I fly and land and lie down, rise on sunstone,
and if I can last, and stroll, somehow last,
even outlast, then there is hope for the gulls

and the bald burren and the dying sticks
walking their dogs thinking they have souls
when all they own is a flat cap, a spring cough
and need for drink every time the darkness tips

its hat into the sea like a dayman; a man
hired on only for one day's work, when the lord
of the manor has so much labour we could have.
I'd want to explode into flamboyant grandeur;

I'd want to summon Babylon's gold hammers.
There are no horses with wings anymore;
and the birds in the air know few emperors;
the stuffing into others that we call sex is

not a wild Atlantic way, but only scuffling;
no final escape in evacuation of bodies;
the gasping for breath as age climbs up
with the burning twenty-year-old is proof;

the world offers no routes of panic for the dying
that do not go through the arms of glassy youth.
I inject, go and sleep in gold pavilions of neglect;
I insert my power into the powerless and come

moaning out the name of my alters, my drum
easily beaten by others. Love the asscurve,
the skincream, the bowdown, the blowjob smile;
and mile by mile Christ staggers across come,

the images of the fluids he rides on we spend;
the world is a burly lost flyer coming down
to tip its flat cap to abandon and words
that spray lacking sinister powers,

won't infest the critical cells; fork nothing
into the caw cawing resonator, the mawstone
where the sea eats broken shells, choking
spawning things that roam and flail among

stones and tides, pools where the trapped
momentarily appear safest in sun.
If love could lift, if language could;
nothing I acted in does that, raises

out of the world; it's all embedding; one loves
the world or one dies in the world; one dies
in the world either way; the source of pain
is the revealing of pain; flimsy glimpse

of juggernaut and old jigging crone;
the famine kitchens tumbled down and left
by the property magnates to spread an image
of dark power; the power of starvation

which we must bring upon ourselves;
otherwise fatten on sunlight and needles;
available sexual images and sloppy suckers;
topple into a bog of alien threnodies;

not all myths are known; foreign hells
are written in a tongue we don't govern.
I want to be the swan that knows lightness
of image, lightness of nobility, that owns

a secret purpose, that breaks out of the word
in its seeming flotation above the jetsam
of a world of sundering magnificence.
Every swan is a matchstick thrown

into the well that bounces on sudden-seen walls
and flashes a warning we are sometimes on fire.
We are fat, lost and free to poison the stuffing;
drink the blood that was given; rebound;

or throttle on puke in the private toilet
and be wound in a white cotton towel,
aimless fat arms riven and exposing
the nails slammed in like fucking;

hate fucking; and wounded
the gliding swanlight
we also can see;
can reveal;

are worldly. In swanlight rise up and be 49.
I do all, I did all
that any may do;
flashing as sun on car bonnets at Heathrow.

Non-payment

A poem is what is tossed aside
by any reader who aims to glide
above rhyme for a novel ride;

I have some words to give freely;
these are words like shooting sprees:
there is no God but the god you leave;

there is no loss but that you grieve;
and it is better to love than live;
though living is what love requires;

the world dampens love's true fires;
for truth and love are not the spires
on which our global good is built;

we rise to worship all that's gilt;
we mourn fewer than get killed;
it is better not to write a lot;

and if you do, try not to shout;
they can hear you even though
you never speak above a slow

mourning whimper, asking how
they know you are so beautiful
and yet they've had their fill

before they've had any at all.
It isn't good but it is the fate
to arrive too early, stay too late

and lean against a burning gate
that soon, low ash, will topple you
for being no more than evening dew;

the night has little else to do
with poems, poets, those who think
their meanings and language sink

ships or move the world to a brink;
the day has even less time for us;
we, to all creation, most useless;

be a doctor, lawyer, good with sums;
bang pots, pans and goat-skin drums;
garden a lot with a prudent thumb;

no green accrues, no gold arrives,
by writing into being what never lives;
the poet dies each time she gives.

the poet dies because she pays a tax
for which no ruler has ever asked;
she tithes and tithes away the mask

until her body, mind and spirit lie
upon a floor that never counted grain
but threshes those who aspire to try

to count each star, each molecule, the ant
across the lintel and the pouring sand;
to enumerate the illiterate plan

nature's laws and Zeus's design;
refrain, resign and diplomatically decline;
the word's unwanted in this flop, this tip.

Knock back a quick one, salute the bar;
where you are going isn't that far;
you'll soon be out the one exact door.

The Heart Of Love Is Of Dark Matter

on her birthday

She recreates the world she begins
when she sings, even though we both
despise Billy Joel, and that's the song
her choir rehearsal requires; a sin

is when what's done is off-piste –
avalanches await those who stray.
I dream bad nightly, wake drained
by guilt for what may have been.

Half of life is wiping the other half clean.
Why division? I crave a simpler union,
not a simpering one. It's the going away
that breaks in two. Going off-course

is creation, bang or garden version.
There's always a bow snapped,
fruit de-branched. Dispersal, no,
need to cohere, crush love down

into a stranger charm, a ball of matter
not slow or massive, a cold core
nonetheless – a hot core that won't slip
or digress. Fall off like a black dress.

I want to build our love as if it was
a model of the working universe
made in a professor's Birmingham office,
all the forces expanding to coalesce.

No longer to be the chaos I contain,
art of madness has flushed my face.
I'm bright toxin, pantaloons on a drunk
performer, torn to bits. Tie me down,

I don't want to flee from you, anymore.
Draw me tightly in, nip the exits please.
Sing the way you do to make my heart spin.
Sing those Irish songs I was born to listen to.

30 March, 2015

What We Knew And When

Ah though we saw the world's fastest man
we shall not be fast
though we read so many books we felt
like paper and thoughts
we are not paper and won't be thought
when we run slowly
over the line that is not book
or track; and when we shared a rose
to compare the scent you had
to the one I had, we knew
neither of us would have such perfume
when we slowly ran into the ground
of brooks and lime and inky soil.
And when we rooted out
our old photographs of being wed,
you all in white, I in magician's black
we counted the guests who were already
dead, not for any lack
on their part, of trying to be otherwise
but just because, as we knew
it did not matter one jot or iota or pin drop
at all at all whatsoever
what we had done or drawn or sang or sewn
or dashed or browned or blued or blown
or ripped or bruised or danced or tongued
or ranged or banged or singed or soiled;
all our toils and when you bothered me
by cleaning my ears out with a pen,
as if my skull was a dirty poem
you wanted to harvest for something
with a nib; we knew, all along, darling

didn't we, as we drew lots
and made lists and paid off debts
(for what, for who, like an owl)
it was all more than vain, it was weak;
it was flimsy, it was a few
seconds of running faster than fast
then eons lying fast in a pine box
where no one talks
about what we never couldn't do
which is go elsewhere better above
such pinions and disappointing news;
we had wanted to park our horses
in a higher, sunnier Mews.

The Shit Show

Basically, Captain, it's a shit show.
It's a shit show of epic proportions.
A real shit show, from the neck down.

No one escapes the shit show.
What a complete shit show.
A first class shit show, all the way up.

Grade A shit show.
The mother of all shit shows.
The shit show to end all shit shows.

No way around it, it's a shit show.
Call the marines, it's a shit show.
A real shit show out there.

Where Said the Grizzly Bear?

The good psychiatrist
with the smile and tie
who would come out of his office
the size of a small yacht
to greet you, the one
who always took your side
in every mad dispute
and also dispensed meds
to pop stars
on the way down,
well, he might soon
be gone.

So too, to be melancholic
about it, let us begin to examine
what has evaporated
from the best of childhood
in your case, Melita,
grandmother of books,
whose name you loved
more than her upbringing:
that severe, five peas until you
eat more, severity.

Christmas
itself is gone, as it happens,
or did – the huge fires
and the big chairs you sat in –
she would bring you
Nabokov and Darwin
as the snow drifted upwards

to reach the second floor;
smack in the Quebec blizzard
like a crow feather;
outside the sugar shacks hunkered
down for spring; the logs
crackled, spat, were alive
as only fires in childhood are;

it was the storm that was staved off
that thrilled; and her collections
of swords and Canadiana.
She was a beauty – whose lips
are ever as red now?
And pale as Laurentian ice.
All gone. How she moved crumbs
cautiously off the table
with a hand while talking
of Layton or Livesay.

Terrible melting away
what is done to us
in the name of causality.
Eminent domain, for what?
A making way for more making way.
The weather is a hurling
occupying force without let up.
Nothing hinders what is coming next.

I speak here of the loss of what else,
but the life that was,
and what it did all day.
I have missed appointments
and kissed the wrong fixations,
but in the end no pearly gates
will station me any closer to

the storm of snow made of zeroes.
You're alone with the big displeasures
of vanishment, little acidities
can be dealt with, the cat hiccups
and bites from gnats; the longer
argument is with the thud of
loss, like snowballs with stones
in them, callously placed there
for extra impact, thrown
from a reckless sleigh.

The bells ring backwards
in the frost moonlight
like mockery from elves.
It is time to go walk into the firs
as if they were a shipwreck;
to set yourself apart from
the onslaught; quietly, circle
in a self-made pit the kindling
as snow falls like angels from a shaken
branch; the angels reach a blank floor.

Expertly set out the whole enveloped calm
equipage of absence ablaze
and lie down by the glow as it settles
down into the melt; a wolf
pack may be just off to the right;
soon you will sleep forever,
after-image of a glowing thing,
of all the rest you knew
to argue among or caress or fear;
lie back in the furred ferny deep sleep
to burn and freeze, once and then again,
as John Whiteside's daughter did.

On My 12th Wedding Anniversary

I left today on an anniversary
of marriage; by bookstore time
was half-dreamy, confused,
passport-missing-manic – no
not an active maniac, a sleepy one
taking me by the hand, to go
astray, as if the picking up
wind was saying, you are no one.
I hide my invisible departure
as well as you probably conceal
your dilemma appetites, the swing
in me is huge, electoral, I am
a gulf between who I think
I may be and who I don't
think anymore at all.
It's a fall, medical in its import,
a Harley street requiring case
at least, impactful, opiatic,
nectarine in its oceanic serenities,
in the way exotic plants thrill
gently; sunsets in blue chlorine;
I am, okay, languidly
out of some slight control,
a breeze gone haywire
off the bend of its protocols
to stir the leaves and rustle
faint murmurations in the grasses;
the pines sway to an emperor
unware he has inherited royalty,
a brained sibling high on parakeet
honey and coconut balderdash;

I am a slapdash bit of the turmoil
in the weather, barely, barely; it
is the subtle apertures into clarity
that scare and appal, if they do;
I am then, imperceptibly
lax, lapsed, a lazy lass and lad
limned with sugaring doubt,
a lonely clouding, instranisgent
intransience, it's all confusing,
really, isn't it, how we waver
in the half-light of our purposes,
diving in and out, porpoises,
needles and thread, all the done
and doing actions, but the mind's
more a dangerous cascade
at a drowning beauty spot
where the falling water thuds
down to take you to a shelf
and you whirl about in your swim
struggling to be free in danger;
I am a voided stub, with a soul,
gone AWOL for a song, a prayer,
I'm long gone, truth to tell, in both
art and tail, tooth and claw,
over the fence, rushed out
across the plain, hopping
the trains rumbling flat out
for some other shabby self,
a coast that costs less, or
I don't know, am I the one
who said yes at the altar,
why twelve years in, just,
do I falter at even who said
that, not a why, but a who
the perplexity here;

bring in the good and bad
to bully me into a confession
but first bring the priest
to balm my head
and name me firmly
for the time being,
again, in the bald light of
the knowledge I am dizzy
and need to sit down,
all of my me needing to
establish a frame
at this point for how we may
go forward, with deliberate speed;
who says there is no spot
change in the leper, the beasts
born able on the veldts
and in the swaying jungles?
We're full spectrum, widely
apart from just one part to play;
I'm all of the above and you,
as well, were married, agreed,
to all of your articles also
back then, when you, dear,
also became a role and walked
down an aisle vibrating
with multiple vocals,
a choir
not a solo,
we do,
we do.

Admonishment

I won't admonish Moses
I wont admonish Aaron
I may admonish roses

I will admonish Charon;
an inspired man,
a man without sons

or daughters, admonish
G-d if you wish,
but sing when the scrolls

walk among us;
lead us to the land
and lead us out of the land;

and lead us through the sea
and do not show us bad TV
but offer us more channels

than ever before;
I have rods, I have comfort,
I have no sons though,

I have no daughters,
but if I had a daughter
I would not want to divide

her share of my inheritance;
I would want my fictional
daughter to have the same

as my fictional son;
but I am not Moses,
I am not Aaron; I am not

a commentary, or a book;
no Rabbi or Cantor
sings for me; I am unlearned;

I am not in the wilderness;
I am not chosen;
I wish to be admonished;

I wish to be chosen;
I wish the fifth part of all
that is done to me be done

to those who would strike me;
I am not a leader
of my people; who are

my people?
These days I admire
those who listen to words

carefully and those who pray
and sing; to those who teach
others to read, pray, and sing.

I admonish no one else
beyond my own false self;
my God I follow slowly

in the sunlight, I am unable
to run anymore, my weariness
is the weariness of

an inspired man without sons
or daughters worrying
about a legacy

that seems not to exist;
my unreal love, my fictive family
I lead about the parks and playgrounds,

the fun fayres, out between
the amusement and the popcorn,
I part the crowds throwing darts

at balloons, I admonish
the smokers near the children,
I admonish the heavens should they open,

I admire Florida from afar
and wonder at the desert, how does it drink?
I am not Moses, I am however mosaic,

I offer no laws; lawless, inspired,
without legacy or offerings, even burnt
offerings, I bear nothing more than

this word list, this book of words,
these layered lines, lawless, yet ordered,
I give them to the people

of the shawl and fedora, the people
of the music and song;
I admonish only that part of myself

which is my enemy; which breaks
the Temple down, always
ten weeks before we celebrate;

Madness And Love In Maida Vale

because only in the ruins
do I find my way; find my son;
and my daughter who doesn't run,

runs out of the rubble to me,
stone by trembling stone,
her limbs light as aches,

unjust as false laws, and she will deserve
all of my inheritance,
all of this which I bring down to you now.

After Reading Wiman's Mandelstam

Easter empties
then gives dividends
like seaspray on lips
a raise to storm level

catcalling blues
Oh my Bombay purrs
youth lights upper candles
with a stretching arm

and we enjoy beautiful
boys in their Christianity
the air like a sea tosses incense
just as a widow tosses

a dark bouquet to the grave
which will marry the ground
to the bone; we are upright
caskets of finery and convey

so many dashing delights
like the lights of St Petersburg,
Paris and May – spring's
outrider, mane shedding blooms

as sweat is a blossom also
to the stallion that runs ahead
of the day
now March renounces Satan

and all the works of sin behind
that grind a waxworks machinery
like villains in an awful play;
kittens have brains a million times

faster than an iPad but smaller
than a sack of marbles:
creature of God your brain folds
and you dart and leap for birds

to ripple on the panthered grass
and turn our yard to junglery.
Turn on the fire, it shoots
from the red gun to teach

darkness how to say thank you.
We cry like gulls at the sea of the grave
which rolls back and opens
white as the empty skill of love

exposing like a perversion its own
smashing waves of desire
on the skull where death is disobeyed.
Lick the rain off her lips

to feel that shivering thrill
of wanting to marry before turning
twenty; your home will be small
and your bed creased by lack

except you will be madly busy kissing
so that even the busy rulers
and busier stars breaking apart
will envy your business in passion.

28 March, 2016

Acknowledgements

Grateful thanks yous are hereby given to all the editors who published, online and/or in print, versions of some of these poems in their journals and magazines, including *The Moth*, and *Blackbox Manifold*.

A special thank you to my friend the poet, artist and book designer Edwin Smet, who has done such a fine job for me here.

·

About the author

Todd Swift was born on Good Friday, 8 April 1966, in Montreal, Quebec, Canada. He is married to the Irishwoman, Sara Egan. He is a poet, anthologist, critic, screenwriter, public speaker, and publisher, based in London, UK. He holds a Phd from the UEA, and was Oxfam GB Poet in residence in 2004. He has had 9 full collections of poetry published, as well as numerous pamphlets; and has edited or co-edited many anthologies. He is both Canadian and British. He is a proud uncle.

Todd Swift, besides being a poet himself,
is one of the most profound advocates
of fine literature – he can smell
depth and relevance!
— Mariela Griffor

.

Todd Swift is a powerhouse editor and poet whose
work crosses boundaries and brings unlikely bedfellows together.
For instance, in his fusion projects, early this century, he had page lie
down with stage and both wake up with a new appreciation of the other.
He has been a generous publisher of my poems in his anthologies,
encouraging my work when such encouragement was needed.
Most of all, his poetry – pop-culture-savvy, historically now,
poetically smart – is to be cherished.
Happy birthday, Todd.
— Patrick Chapman

.

Todd Swift has been a force for good in
poetry for 30 years and has tirelessly supported
many poets who are just starting out, myself included.
Here's to the next 30 years!
— Ben Parker

.

There's a questing generosity and vulnerability
in Todd Swift's poems that allows him to venture into emotional
territory that less ambitious poets shy away from. His is not a poetry that
seeks acceptance within the safe lines of current literary fashion. Rather
he has set his own distinct course absorbing and transforming quite
variant cultural influences into a consistently engaging body of work.
The fact that his generosity as a poet has always paralleled his equal
devotion as an anthologist, teacher of literature, and curator
of reading series is all the more cause to celebrate this
first half century of his work.
— Robert Priest

The first time I met Todd Swift
was in his apartment and he made me a cup of tea and asked
me if I wanted honey in it, so I said, yeah, honey would be great. The
second time I met Todd Swift was in an Italian restaurant and it was
Shrove Tuesday so we ate cannelloni and it was a bit dry. I think we had a
conversation about A. Alvarez and I said that I loved his book on Beckett.
Todd was the only person who was particularly enthusiastic about my
work when it got shortlisted for the Forward Prize. The third time I met
Todd Swift was in the Marylebone Oxfam Bookshop where he ran a great
poetry series. I also met Stephen Gyllenhaal, who was trying his hand
at poetry, and I gushed about the episodes of Twin Peaks he'd directed:
the only good episodes of season 2, something I don't think he ever gets
enough credit for. In the basement, which is the same size as the shop
floor, but like a bad dream about a bookshop or some kind of
Bosch overlay you could put over the top of a bookshop,
Todd gave me a copy of Encounter, the poetry magazine funded
by the CIA. The issue was pink and orange, like a Fruit
Salad chew and I still have it facing outwards in my office.
— Luke Kennard

·

Todd Swift is 50 now, and I've just turned 52.
He began his career in poetry exactly 30 years ago. I began my
career in poetry exactly 30 years ago. We share a love of poetry from the
1940s. We're exact contemporaries! Todd is a discerning force in poetry
today, a scholar, and a fine poet as well. I am personally grateful to him
for championing my poems on his fantastic Eyewear blog; and we are all
grateful to him for providing a home and base for so many poets to find
their way and their deserved audiences with his terrific series of Eyewear
books as a publisher. We all wish him the very best as he begins the
second half of his life, the richest and best part of all, and rightly so.
And we look forward to the many future surprises he undoubtedly
has in store for us. Cheers to Todd!
— Ben Mazer

·

A warm, enthusiastic and generous person,
Todd Swift has been renowned on the British poetry scene since
I became aware of such thing. At times eccentric and controversial (all the
best people are), Todd – like his own poetry – is energetic, multifaceted
and always surprising, yet he is also a tireless and dedicated
supporter of poetry and fellow poets. I couldn't have a
more considerate (and stylish!) editor.
— Marion McCready

·

You might call it a McGarrett, but super, smashing
great Todd's scored a bullseye.
—Tim Wells

·

Todd Swift's dedication to poetry is built on his
unfailing passion, incredible knowledge and stalwart exuberance.
In creating Eyewear he has set himself at the vanguard of publishing new
poetry and deserves wide-ranging recognition. I was proud to have been
Todd's first UK publisher at tall lighthouse with his engaging collection
Mainstream Love Hotel and equally proud to have worked with
him on the successful 20/20 pamphlet series. Long may he
flourish on the UK poetry publishing scene...
Many happy returns...
— Les Robinson

·

Doctor Swift's fertility –
Defying sterility –
Is firmly seminal;
He jets and squirts word-shaped inks,
Mocking Genesis as jinx,
In poems gelled eternal.
— George Elliott Clarke

·

If Todd Swift had not existed in all his web savvy wonderfulness,
British Poetry would still be conducting itself in the back rooms of
The Old Dog and Duck ...
— Tony Lewis-Jones

Todd Swift has spent a lifetime writing, editing and
championing poetry on a scale that few can match.
He is the man who removed 12 poems from my debut
collection, some of which I'd worked on for years.
He did so in the way he does most things; with an open heart
and an unshakeable conviction that he was in the right...
I REALLY wanted him to be wrong...
He REALLY wasn't...
He rarely is.
— Keiran Goddard

•

Poet, mentor, publisher, innovator, editor, critic, intellectual,
collaborator, performer, blogger, anthologist, friend, shaker-upper, a
Canadian swallowtail, a British purple emperor, a monarch, a creative
force of nature: these are all the Todd Swifts I love and admire.
— Mel Pryor

•

Todd Swift is both an accomplished poet *and*
an insightful publisher.
— Jessie Lendennie

•

We drank coffee in
Todd's yard. The sun was blinding,
but he helped me see.
— Andrew Shields

•

Todd is an egg. By that I mean he is good.
Good tutor, good poet, good editor, good friend.
— Laura Guthrie

•

I heard you read at Ben McNally's bookstore
in Toronto, enjoyed it immensely and bought and read the book
When All My Disappointments Came At Once has much to recommend it.
The title poem, for starters, is not only a wonderfully clever conceit,
but derives much of its authority from the delicate click of recurring
consonants and the sonority of open vowels. I recall being impressed with
your ear and fine narrative gift, so evident in 'Michael Kolhass' and some
of the shorter pieces. I also remember being amused by the perception
in 'Love or Poetry' of the urge many poets have, after the pressures of the
form, to "swim in prose," where less is required and where there are too
many words to keep track of, never mind whip into appropriate shape.
Some say a poet is lucky to produce a dozen lasting poems in a lifetime.
You're obviously well on your way. — Gary Geddes

•

The tenderness in his poetic voice speaks
Of all the pains and joys of yesterdays with a prolific dignity where
Downfall is defeated with the hindsight of compassion. Each
Decision is versed by the cadence of a kind reflecting

Soul. His poetry is a brilliant balance of rhetorical glamour,
Wit, sometimes comical timing, self-reflection, and
Innovation that forces us to question our state of reality and
Faith. His body of work is important to humanity because it represents
Those things that matter to us the most that need to be talked about.
— Guiseppe Bartoli

Lightning Source UK Ltd.
Milton Keynes UK
UKOW01f0719080416

271829UK00002B/21/P